Little Pebble™

Our Families

T0100963

Mothers Are Part of a Family

by Lucia Raatma

CAPSTONE PRESS
a capstone imprint

Little Pebble is published by Capstone Press,
1710 Roe Crest Drive, North Mankato, Minnesota 56003
www.mycapstone.com

Copyright © 2018 by Capstone Press, a Capstone imprint. All rights reserved.
No part of this publication may be reproduced in whole or in part, or stored in a retrieval system, or transmitted in any form or by any means, electronic, mechanical, photocopying, recording, or otherwise, without written permission of the publisher.

Library of Congress Cataloging-in-Publication Data is available on the Library of Congress website

ISBN: 978-1-5157-7465-5 (library binding)
ISBN: 978-1-5157-7473-0 (paperback)
written by Lucia Raatma

Editorial Credits
Christianne Jones, editor; Juliette Peters, designer;
Wanda Winch, media researcher; Laura Manthe, production specialist

Photo Credits
Capstone Studio: Karon Dubke, 5, 7, 9, 13, 15, 19, 21; Shutterstock: Angelina Babii, paper texture, Dubova, 17, Monkey Business Images, cover, Photographee.eu, 11, Syda Productions, 1, Teguh Mujiono, tree design

Printed in the United States 5329

Table of Contents

Mothers 4

What Mothers Do 8

Glossary 22

Read More 23

Internet Sites 23

Index 24

Mothers

A mother has children.

She is a parent.

Some mothers are called mom. Some are called mama.

What Mothers Do

Cam plays piano.

His mom helps.

Rayan's mom works in an office. She is busy.

Luca's mom builds houses.

She works hard.

TS GROUP
PRELIMINARY

Thomas and his mom bake. They love cookies!

SOTO
EXTRA VIRGIN

Bria's moms like to be outside. Bria does too.

Anna feels sick. Her mom gives her medicine.

Mothers snuggle.

Mothers kiss.

Mothers love.

Glossary

bake—to cook in an oven

mama—another name for mom

medicine—a pill or treatment for healing an illness

office—a place where people go to work

parent—a mother or father

snuggle—to hold close

Read More

Harris, Robie H. *Who's in My Family?* All bout Our Families. Somerville, MA: Candlewick, 2012.

Lewis, Clare. *Familes Around the World.* Mankato, MN: Heinemann-Raintree, 2015.

Simon, Norma. *All Kinds of Families.* Park Ridge, IL: Albert Whitman & Company, 2016.

Internet Sites

FactHound offers a safe, fun way to find Internet sites related to this book. All of the sites on FactHound have been researched by our staff.

Here's all you do:
Visit *www.facthound.com*
Type in this code: 9781515774655

Index

baking, 14

building, 12

giving medicine, 18

kissing, 20

loving, 20

outside, 16

parents, 4

playing piano, 8

sickness, 18

snuggling, 20

working, 10